THE RAVEN CHRONICLES

PERNOD
ABSINTHE

DAVID A. BAINBRIDGE

THE RAVEN CHRONICLES

Cover, illustrations and text design: David A. Bainbridge and David Wogahn

RIO REDONDO PRESS

Rio Redondo Press Mission: Advancing sustainability accounting and reporting, increasing sustainable management of resources and people, and protecting future generations.

ISBN 978-1-7351492-0-2

Manufactured in the United States of America 2021

TO L WITH ALL MY LOVE

Table of Contents

Being Raven

A raven doesn't walk
It struts
A purposeful side to side stride
Or energetic skip/hops
It is a raven's world
After all

Old Friends

Snowshoes lift the powder snow
And the wind carries it across the trail
As the hunter moves up the canyon
The swish, swish sound gladdens the heart
As hoar frost sparkles in the sun
In a meadow ahead, *tatanka*
But the old buffalo need not fear the hunter
As he comes closer he sees *kangee* (the raven)
Standing on the buffalo's back
The hunter smiles
All the people in his band know this pair
Together for many years
After *kangee* lost his wife and family in a violent hail storm
He met the bull, wounded and near death
Driven out by a younger, stronger bull
Raven talked with him as the bull's wounds healed
Raven talks all the time, but the buffalo listens well
Now *kangee* is so old he can barely fly
Feathers tattered and dull
One eye has grown dim
He rides more often than flies
Tatanka is old beyond old
But *kangee* helps keep him safe from the wolves
Together each day
They watch the sun rise
The clouds dance across the sky
And the stars come out
Here in the land of the Lakota

Dumpster Diving

Ravens are cautious
By nature
The lowest power raven gets to test
New foods
Like the King's taster of old
But a dumpster
Can entice even the wise old raven
With caution offset by
Curiosity
Like kids after piñata candy
Ravens will
Dive into dumpsters
Who knows what treasures await
Within

Raven Waltz

The moist south wind runs up the eroded sandstone
Providing lift for the ravens
Dancing in the morning light
Two pairs, swinging gentle figure eights
First he leads, then she leads, tight turns
The pairs overlap, then apart
Imagining their conversation
How many years or decades together
To get the timing just right, each pair turning as one
With an occasional dip or rise
Or legs and feet dropped down to touch the bird beneath
I watch for ten minutes and then
    as I get closer the dance ends
And they slide downwind to the point

The Small and the Righteous

Ravens bully each other
Hawks, owls, and other predators too
And many others when the mood strikes them
Why? Because they can...
Malicious fun
But the tables can be turned
The young raven still had his learner's permit
When he crossed into hummingbird territory
At Torrey Pines
It was no contest
The micromite buzzed and zoomed
And drove the raven down into the bushes
It perched for a second, lost balance and fell
Flapping through the branches to the ground
Hunched over and cawing for his parents
"Help, help, save me, save me"
They didn't hear, or were too embarrassed to intervene
The hummer swooped wild victory loops
The black bully was beat down
For the moment

Spring Fling

The word went out
Torrey Pines, March 2
More than forty ravens
Came and took part
The last great social event
Of Spring
Nest building starts soon
And too soon after that
Eggs, sitting, minding
Hatching and never ending work
Feeding the youngsters
But this day is for play
Speed dating
Romancing
Enjoying long term partners
In dances traced across the sky
Busting loose
After winter's
Longer, cool nights
Amazing aerials, waltzes, tangos and quick steps
Two by two or sometimes
Three by two and chases
Who gets the pretty girl
Or who is the best flier
Or singer
Total chaos
Flying through the trees with abandon
Circling high in a mass raven host

Dives and spins and flips
Then swooping down to perch and talk
Perhaps reflecting on years gone by
Or the state of the raven economy
By days end it is quiet
The next morning
A few more ravens than usual
Are hanging around
Perhaps hoping to find a mate
Or just hung over from the party
And then they too are gone

The Old Couple

They nestle near a crook of the ancient, twisted pine
Close together, with a beak touch now and again
Big, but a bit tattered, black
An old couple
They murmur, craw, and "clck" to each other
Subdued and gentle sounds for ravens
A quiet conversation
Forty years together
What do they talk about?
Adventures, children, grandchildren
The great feasts and great hungers
Or nuzzling, murmuring sweet nothings now
Simply content

Terminal Velocity

Ravens are competitive
And the two brothers were no exception
Always trying to outdo
The other
As they learned to fly
They tried the hardest tricks
The flips, reversals
Flying upside down
Perhaps the speed contests
Were inevitable
After all
They had seen the peregrine dive
Down the cliff
At 200 miles an hour
Could ravens go that fast?
The brothers would find out
Further up and faster down
They flew
Side by side
Pushing the limits
Of strength and ability
Day by day higher then faster
Until
In the red light of a falling sun
They dove down the cliff

Faster than ever before
Neither would pull out
Until they realized that
Their wings could not be extended
Into the racing wind
They died
As teenagers too often do
Learning the limits
Of speed and pride

Tumbling Ravens

The sandstone fin is rich reddish tan
A strong steady wind hits head on,
Funneled up the steep face
A gang of ravens play tumbledore in the blast
Circling around behind the fin
Cruising low, slow and flat over the top of the fin
Into the blast and flipping over and over
As they bounce up into the sky
Dropping down
They swing around
For another tumble
Is it a bunch of teenage ravens out for fun?
Or is this a family outing?
So many questions, so few answers
But great delight in sharing the time
With the playful and engaging
Stunt flyers

Thirst

So thirsty
So hot
Feathers fluffed
Panting
What folly led me out
To the east
A hard days flying
Against the wind
Has me back to familiar ground
No luck
Finding water
Even the rock pockets in box canyon were dry
The *cienaga* too
Shade of the ironwood helps
But so hot
So thirsty
Panting
Waiting for the north wind to stop
No lift
No life
Day to night to day
So thirsty
Panting
Hot
Now feel it
The wind turns
To the east
Just enough will left

For a hop from the branch
A few wing beats
Feel the rising air
Wind against the rock face
So thirsty
Extended feathers for maximum lift
Turning, following
The rising column of air
So thirsty
Rising faster now
Up the ridges
The top
In view, green trees
So thirsty
Turning and rising
Minimal energy left
Survive....
Looking intently
For the sparkle of water
Or dark wet ground
So thirsty
Rising higher crossing the pass
Then
The flash of reflection
On water
Gliding down
Caution cast aside
Barely enough strength to
Flare out, Splash,Ahh....

Snorre (The Unruly One)

As dawn broke over the shore
The *drekar* were muscled up the shingle beach
Footsteps crunching, armor and shields on
The brittle sound of ice sheets breaking
A bit of fish and meat to eat with hot berry broth
Men talking, shouting, cursing, praying
Horses, breathing hard, come ashore from the *snarrs*
Excited as well, nostrils flared
But the tides turn
As sunset approaches
Snorre lies in the cold field of snow and mud
Bloodied, unable to move
A sword blow to the head and neck
Dying
The large raven approaches
A steady but watchful walk
He has seen this all before
Peering into the iron mask and dimming blue eyes
Snorre laughs and calls out, "*Welcome muninn,*
Soon enough you will eat well,
But wait awhile
I will see the stars
And remember the sun"
Valhalla awaits

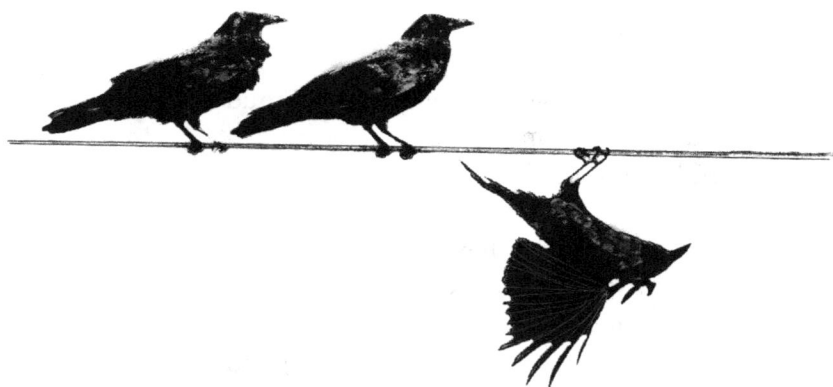

Like a Bird On The Wire

Dad, mom, junior
One guess
Junior isn't quite the doofus
He may appear
He is learning a trick
Many ravens know
Perched on the wire
Relax the grip
Spin upside down
A deft flick of the wings
Back up again
Junior doesn't quite
Have it yet
And is flapping away
But he will
Master the trick
And move on to the next

Landfall

The mist thickens as dusk approaches
Sounds muffled by the fog
The slap of waves rolling by
Men's breath condenses
Waiting, watching, after weeks at sea
Which way is land?
High cirrus the afternoon before
Portent of approaching storm
Erik calls forward,
"Loose the ravens"
Gydri the far flying and
Brud the younger lift off
Wing beats loud in the quiet
They rise in a steady circle
At the limit of sight Brud returns
Perching on the sternpost, quiet, downcast
Gone from sight
Higher and higher Gydri circles
As she has done many times over
Twenty years
Then suddenly she appears
Slices low across the ship
Straight as an arrow
About 30 degrees off the bow
Tok, tok, tok—follow me
Erik pulls the steering oar over,
"All right you insolent loafing bastards,
Oars out and pull!"

Every few minutes Gydri returns
Checking the course
Repeats the slow straight glide
Providing a clear line to follow
Hearing waves break
All pause, then slow ahead
Until the faint outline of land
Appears out of the mist
With a triumphant *tok, tok*
Gydri lands on Erik's shoulder
And gets a treat
Brud "the timid", complains
From the masthead
Still young, he may yet learn
To be a pathfinder

Dog Tag

The parking lot was quiet
Until the dog arrived
Unleashed
A Samoyed cross
With a flourish
The raven landed close
In full view
A furious charge
The raven a'-wing
Hopping just out of reach
Looking intently at the dog
If ravens had lips, it would be smiling
The dog charges again, again, and again
All to no avail
Skills honed teasing wolves over millennia
The dog, exhausted, relents
The raven chuckles to himself
And strides confidently down the parking lot
Back turned to the dog
Black, shiny, and proud

Arctic Raven

Cold, cold wind
Greets *tulugaq* as he steps out of the snow pocket
That provided shelter last night
A quick hop and aloft, currents kicked
    up by the pressure ridge
Faint and far away
The sound of dogs, excited
Being tied into a fan trace
Soon know
The light load means hunting, not travel
Tulugaq dips low over the hunter
"Rawk, rawk, rawk" (Greetings friend)
"Let's find a natchiq (hair seal)
And eat"
The team races across the ice
As *"Nanuq"* (nickname the bear) runs behind
Tulugaq scans the ice
Looking for movement, or a breathing hole
But just a *qujhaa* (fox), white on white
Then movement, dark and large, *natchiq*
Tulugaq drops down in front of the team
And leads the hunter in
The stalk, the wait, the kill
The harpoon of *Nanuq*
Takes the seal
Quickly cut and packed
Many small pieces of heart and blubber left
The team is harnessed, ready to run
Nanuq calls to the raven,
"Eat well my friend, look for me again
So we may hunt and eat together"

Battle Rattle

The ravens know that sound
The distant clamor
Shields and swords
Axes
Battle rattle
Horses running
Voices raised
In command
In rage
In fear
The screams
Of the wounded
Foretell
The feast to come

Cliff Climbers

Ravens climbing the cliff face
Surprising, but not
Ravens are a remarkable lot
A very steep face
But foot by foot
With an occasional outside wing beat
Or beak hold
They climb the sandstone cliff
Something to eat there?
Or simply an interesting challenge
With ravens
You never know

Chutes and Ladders

A lovely winter day in Zion
Red rock fins and slabs bright in the sun
Thousands of feet
We see the ravens working
Up the cliffs
Not much lift on this cold day
Every pass along the cliff
Provides a small gain
Back and forth
Flying precise patterns
To gain as much as possible
Twenty minutes
And it is done
Topping out
The ravens are off
To some new
Adventure

The Raven Mafiusu

I walk the beach at Torrey Pines almost every day
And over the years I was befriended by a raven
As I sat on Bathtub Rock watching the sea roll in
I shared my snacks with him
He already spoke a few words of Human
And once I learned some Raven
We talked about life
Friends, family, food, the beauty of a sunset
One day our talk turned to the Raven community
"Little Mike" said it was pretty straightforward
Bound by tradition, power, and will
Just like he imagined human communities might be
He went on to say that the ravens divvy things up in January
    (with some midyear corrections)
Before the nests are built, refurbished, and eggs are laid
A series of meetings, squabbles, beat downs and negotiations
Determine the rights to shopping centers,
    fast food dumpsters, and other hot spots
The riches go to the big, fast, powerful
Swagger, pride, bully and bluff
Tempered by the size of the group
Led by either a male or female
A mean bully without many friends may not
Do as well as a strong but kind leader
With committed followers
Families and relations often work together
Older ravens get respect from the younger
In part because they are big and strong

But also because of what they have learned
Over the decades
Starting at Torrey Pines, the area he knows best
He laid out the current alignment
The parking lot area is run by Big Mike
        (his grandfather) and Julia
Not as valuable as when the Kuumeyaay village was nearby
Relations with humans were better then—
But still a good resource
Big Mike and Julia still build a nest
        in the cliff slot site each year
But are beyond chick rearing age
Little Mike and Debbie have a nest site in the mud hills
Of south Torrey Pines not far away
And usually fledge two or three youngsters a year
That their grandparents sometimes baby sit
South of them is the Glider Port, a rich resource
Run by a gang of young hooligans
Not quite old enough to set up a nest or pair up
Nothing but trouble, he admits with a sigh
Tom Wolfe could write a book about them...
The UCSD ravens (another youth gang) are just south of them
And together they have seemingly endless parties and brawls
Then you get down into the city
The La Jolla Shores clan keeps a close watch on the beach
All the way from Scripps to the Cove
To the east a small family controls La Jolla Village Square
And spreading out to the east and south
A network of interconnected, interrelated
        raven families, clans and gangs
Probably about 6,000 for the whole city he guesses

Tho' ravens aren't so good with big numbers
And when a community meeting is called
It is usually regional
Sixty or more ravens may gather from the surrounding area
To hash things out
Raven pride can lead to long-term feuds
But generally things are settled with a maximum of noise
And posturing but a minimum of physical violence
So as you travel through the city
Keep an eye out for the local ravens
Watch the joy they get from life
We could all learn from them
*Sicilian—swagger, root of mafioso

The All Blacks

The winter winds blew cold
Across the Yellowstone River
With drifting snow
The sparkle of hoar frost
In the air
And the sound of ice, tinkling in
The open sections of the water
But the ravens were content
Full of elk from a recent wolf kill
And warmed by the hot spring
They gathered around
The younger ravens rested
And the elder raven recounted the tale
Of how ravens became —All black
"In the beginning….," She said
The great raven created the earth
And saw that it was good
And she created little raven in her image
All white, A sparkling brilliant white
Like fresh snow in the sun
And to keep raven entertained and fed
She created wolf, and fox, and bear
Deer, elk and rabbit
And all the other creatures
And to keep raven from becoming too prideful
She created eagle, even bigger and stronger
Than raven
But ravens were not easily humbled

They were smart and bold
And soon learned how to tease the eagle
And whenever eagles were seen
Ravens would gather
To crowd, harass and tease them
Until one day
The ravens chased a great white eagle
The eagle circled higher and higher
First in the thermals rising off the mountain slope
Then catching the updraft of a giant thunder cloud
And still the ravens followed
And teased the eagle
The eagle screamed in frustration
Just as you hear eagles scream today
Higher and higher they flew
Until they approached the sun
Hotter and hotter
Yet still the ravens rose above and dove on the eagle
They were absorbed in the game
Not noticing the heat burning their feathers
First a few singe marks
And then black edges and more
Even after the frustrated eagle dove back to earth
Cooling its head and tail in the wind
The ravens rose higher squawking in triumph
And so, even today
The bald eagle is black with a white head and tail
But the ravens who had flown higher
Were black, All black

Rave

A strong southwest wind creates a strong uplift
Off the glider port cliffs
Party time for the ravens
Twenty or more tweenagers by their size
Are having an exuberant mixer
Who spread the word that today was the day?
Swooping and tumbling through the air
Flips, dives, rising fast on gusts
Upside down flying and touching toes
Raising a ruckus
Is it a rave or raven meet and greet?
Are partners considered, tested
Who is cutest, most clever, bold, shy?
All wearing the same suit of black
But still so different
Or are they simply enjoying the joy of flight
And more serious matters will wait

Beach Walk

Mid-morning Torrey Pines beach
The old couple walk up the beach
Picking through the flotsam
Now and again
Something interesting to pick up or test
Now and again
Something to eat
We wonder, as we walk
If the old ravens find it
As satisfying as we do?

Ski Jump

The skittering sound
Was unique, what was it?
Looking around
I finally found the source
A couple of ravens were skiing down
A metal roof
Around and around they went
Landing on the roof peak
The hopping off onto the steeply sloped metal
Skiing down the roof, skittering claw feet
and then
Opening wings, flying up
For another run
Let 'er rip!

Raven Loves Eggs

Raven saw the rafters and kayakers
Long before they saw her
They drifted down the Owyhee together
When they pulled out
And left for a hike
Raven went to work
First pull off the loose rain cover
Then unzip the zipper
Pull out the first food bag
Pull out the second
Unseal the bag
Drag out the carton
Of eggs
Break egg and enjoy
Gather egg in mouth and fly over
The hikers
Watch them
Wonder where the egg came from
Soon they will find out
Ravens love eggs
Ravens are smart
Ravens are clever
Ravens love eggs

The Fallen

The black shapes gather
Dark figures in the bare branches
Of the tree
Quiet for a change
They sit close together
Below in the snow
A fallen comrade
After a few minutes
The wake is over
And quietly they depart
Only the wing beats break
The silence

Nevermore

he who writes the history tells the tale
whether it be true or not
i was the raven poe immortalized
his telling of the story was half true
at best
i was not some stranger
he knew me well in fact
having shared many an evening together
outside his little shack
we met first at mount tom
where he sat alone
it started with just a bit of bread at first
i felt sorry for the man
sad eyes, mustache and sighs
i cheered him up as he drank
with tales of my own misspent youth
along the hudson and in the gangs of new york
as time went on, his sadness struck me as well
and i started to nip some beer and later
the green white absinthe
the sweetness and bitterness fit a raven's taste
the louche a treat
until the day of which he wrote
an old acquaintance met
and as i waited his return
i sipped and sipped again
ravens can hold their liquor
as anyone can attest

but absinthe is another story still
tipsy, falling, hallucinating flailing wings
i left
crash landed in the street
narrowly missed by the large feet of a draft horse
and crushing iron wagon wheel
i flailed and flapped down the alley
slept it off in a bush
behind a bar on amsterdam avenue
oh the headache and remorse
to continue with this folly
with headache raging flew to his domicile
perched upon the bust of pallas
i made it clear, "nevermore"
we parted ways
and in a fit he wrote
to cast me in an evil light
the source of his despair
the truth is clear, when facts are known
t'was he the villain
the story told the listener hears
what happened then
and nevermore

transcribed by david a bainbridge

About Ravens

Ravens (*Corvus corax*[1]) are large, intelligent, playful birds that prosper in environments ranging from arid deserts to arctic cold. Often considered scavengers, ravens are effective hunters that cooperate with humans and other species. They are omnivores and enjoy many of the same foods we do. Captive birds have shown a preference for chips, burgers, and other junk food.

Ravens may live 30–40 years (or more), much longer than other birds. Their long life, stable relationships, and cleverness led them to be featured in many tribal stories, often as a trickster. In Norse mythology, two ravens, Muninn (emotion and desire) and Huginn (thought), perched on Odin's shoulders. Odin was also known as the Raven God, Hrafnaguð.

Pair bonds are long-lasting and some pairs have been spotted together for more than twenty years. Their social relationships are complex and complicated. Most commonly seen as pairs or parents with youngsters, in some areas they spend the winter in flocks to forage in the day and roost together at night. They are also known to have festivals, where ravens gather in spring or summer—perhaps just to socialize.

Ravens exhibit a wide range of vocalizations, from the traditional "rok, rok, rok" to pops, clicks, burbles, and many other sounds. They are good mimics and can learn to speak, as Poe's raven did (with a considerable vocabulary). They may be able to combine words to express new concepts. Friends report existence of a pair in the northern woods that have learned to perfectly mimic the sound of the backup alarm on timber harvesting equipment.

Ravens build large, untidy nests of sticks that may be 3–4 feet across, often on ledges or cliffs, but also in trees and on buildings. A clutch of three or more eggs are laid after mating at age 3 or 4.

---

[1] Ravens are larger than their black cousins, the crows. The raven tail is curved while the crow's is square. Ravens also have bigger beaks.

Depending on food resources, most will fledge, thanks to attentive care from the parents. The large chicks are dependent for several months, and it takes a while for them to learn to fly well and hunt for food.

Watching ravens can be very entertaining. They enjoy a wide range of play, including interspecies games of tag. They are superb stunt flyers capable of performing flips, spins, loops, paired aerobatics (sometimes one flying upside down with interlocked talons), and other amusing behaviors. I have also seen them engage in stunt speed-flying through tree canopies (no doubt, the teenagers). Ravens often exhibit these acrobatic skills in pre-nesting seasons where sky dancing is part of the bonding process.

As with any charismatic species, there are many papers and books about ravens, but I would suggest the following.

- Heinrich, B. 1999. *Mind of the Raven: Investigations and Adventures with Wolf-Birds.* Cliff Street Books, New York.
- Fraser, ON and T Bugnyar. 2010. The quality of social relationships in ravens. *Animal Behavior* 79:927-933.
- Fraser ON and T Bugnyar. 2010. Do ravens show consolation? Responses to distressed others. *PLoS ONE* 5(5): e10605. doi:10.1371/journal.pone.0010605.
- Kristan, WB, W I Boarman and JJ Crayon. 2004. Diet composition of common ravens across the urban-wildland interface of the West Mojave Desert. *Wildlife Society Bulletin* 32(1):244–253.
- Stahler, D, B Heinrich, DW Smith. 2002. The raven's behavioral association with wolves. *Animal Behavior.* 64:283-290.
- Sullivan, A. 2003. Raven Summer—lessons learned from the birds. *Alaska Fish and Wildlife News.* October. http://www.adfg.alaska.gov/index.cfm?adfg=wildlifenews.view_article&articles_id=49&issue_id=7
- Wright, J, RE Stone and N Brown. 2003. Communal roosts as structured information centers in the raven, Corvus corax. *Journal of Animal Ecology.* 72:103-1014.

About the Author

David A. Bainbridge grew up in the west, spending his formative years in a small town east of the Cascade Mountains (population 354) in northern Washington. After earning a BA in Earth Sciences, he completed an MS in Ecology. He worked as a consultant on geological resources, passive solar design, and community design for resource conservation for several years. He also conducted research on straw bale building systems and taught workshops on bale building. He returned to academia and worked on desert and dryland restoration from 1981–2021 at the University of California, Riverside's Drylands Research Institute; San Diego State; Alliant International University; and as a consultant. His special focus was on understanding the impacts of disturbance, low-cost restoration, and super-efficient irrigation systems for remote sites. He finished his academic career teaching management, ecological economics, ethics, cultural geography, and environmental science.

David's poems have been published in several newspapers and magazines. This is his second book of poetry, following *Waterglass* (1979). He lives in San Diego, CA.

Other books by the author:
The Straw Bale House (1994)
A Guide to Desert and Dryland Restoration (2007)
Passive Solar Architecture (2011)
Gardening with Less Water (2015)
Fur War: 1765–1840 (2 volumes; 2020, 2021)

Many other books, book chapters, and dozens of papers on dryland and desert restoration, eco-agriculture, solar design and agroforestry can also be found.

For more information, visit
http://works.bepress.com/david_a_bainbridge
www.furwar.com

www.ingramcontent.com/pod-product-compliance
Lightning Source LLC
Chambersburg PA
CBHW050604280326
41933CB00011B/1981